THE SCIENCE BEHIND

Sport

Chris Oxlade

www.raintreepublishers.co.uk
Visit our website to find out
more information about
Raintree books.

To order:
☎ Phone 0845 6044371
🖹 Fax +44 (0) 1865 312263
🖳 Email myorders@raintreepublishers.co.uk

Customers from outside the UK please telephone +44 1865 312262

Raintree is an imprint of Capstone Global Library
Limited, a company incorporated in England and
Wales having its registered office at 7 Pilgrim
Street, London, EC4V 6LB – Registered company
number: 6695582

Text © Capstone Global Library Limited 2012
First published in hardback in 2012
The moral rights of the proprietor have been
asserted.

Edited by Claire Throp, Megan Cotugno,
    and Vaarunika Dharmapala
Designed by Steve Mead
Original illustrations © Capstone Global Library
    Ltd 2012
Illustrations by Oxford Designers & Illustrators
Picture research by Ruth Blair
Originated by Capstone Global Library Ltd
Printed and bound in China by Leo Paper
    Products Ltd

ISBN 978 1 406 23410 7 (hardback)
16 15 14 13 12 11
10 9 8 7 6 5 4 3 2 1

British Library Cataloguing in Publication Data
Oxlade, Chris
The science behind sport
796'.015-dc22
A full catalogue record for this book is available
from the British Library.

Acknowledgements
We would like to thank the following for
permission to reproduce photographs: Corbis
pp. **11** (© JLP/Jose L. Pelaez), **17** (© Duane Osborn/
Somos Images), **21** (© Manuel Blondeau/Photo &
Co.); Getty Images pp. **8** (Sam Bloomberg-Rissman/
Blend Images), **13** (Jacques Demarthon/AFP), **20**
(Cameron Spencer), **23** (Jeffrey Coolidge/Iconica);
Photolibrary p. **19** (Matt Hage/Alaskastock);
Shutterstock pp. **5** (© Martin Valigursky), **7**
(© Poulsons Photography), **10** (© Dusan Zidar),
12 (© Amy Myers), **15** (© Dennis Sabo), **16**
(© Maryunin Yury Vasilevich), **18** (© Dainis Derics),
22 (© Galina Barskaya), **25** (© Benis Arapovic).

Cover photograph reproduced with permission
of Shutterstock (© Schmid Christophe).

We would like to thank Nancy Harris for her
invaluable help in the preparation of this book.

Contents

Look for these boxes:

Stay safe
These boxes tell you how to keep yourself and your friends safe from harm.

In your day
These boxes show you how science is a part of your daily life.

Measure up!
These boxes give you some fun facts and figures to think about.

Some words appear in bold, **like this**. You can find out what they mean by looking at the green bar at the bottom of the page or in the glossary.

Science in sport

What **sport** do you enjoy playing? Perhaps it is football, or tennis, or gymnastics, or running, or swimming? Do you enjoy playground games with your friends?

Have you ever thought about the science that is going on when you play sport and games?

Science in movement

During playground games, you often run about, jump up and down, and throw balls to each other. Science is at work all the time when you are running, jumping, throwing, and catching.

Science explains how you start and stop, move up and down, throw a ball and catch it again, and lots more.

In your day

Next time you play a throwing and catching game in the playground, think about the science of how a ball goes up and down. You push on the bottom of the ball to throw it up. A **force** called **gravity** pulls down on the ball. Gravity makes the ball stop going up, and then fall back down again.

sport	activity that needs fitness or skill
force	push or pull that makes things move

What makes you jump? Why does running make you tired? What makes a ball fall to the ground? Science can answer all these questions!

gravity   force that pulls things down to the ground

Moving your body

Imagine you are jumping up to catch a basketball. How do you make yourself jump? You use your **skeleton** and **muscles**. First you bend your legs. Then you make them straight again ... and up you go!

Your skeleton is your body's frame. It is made of bones. It supports all the other parts of your body. There are **joints** between your skeleton's bones. For example, your elbow is the joint between the bones in your upper arm and your lower arm. Joints let your arms, legs, back, and other parts of your skeleton bend.

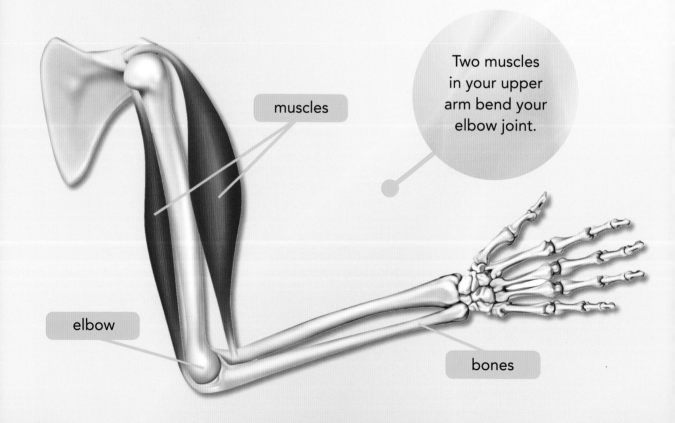

muscles

Two muscles in your upper arm bend your elbow joint.

elbow

bones

skeleton   frame of bones that supports your body
muscle   part of your body that makes your skeleton bend and move

Muscles

Muscles make your skeleton move. Making your muscles shorter and longer makes your joints bend. For example, the muscles in your upper leg make your knee bend.

This athlete has strong muscles that allow him to lift heavy weights.

Stay safe

Sportspeople such as runners, swimmers, and footballers always exercise just before they race or play. This gets their muscles working. This exercise is called warming up. An athlete who does not warm up properly can easily injure a muscle.

Breathing and blood

Imagine you are running in a race. What happens to your body after a few seconds of running? You start breathing faster and taking bigger breaths. Your heart starts beating faster.

Your muscles need **oxygen** to work. Oxygen is a **gas** that comes from the air. When you breathe, air goes into your **lungs**. Inside your lungs, oxygen goes from the air into your blood. Your heart pumps the blood from your lungs to your muscles.

When you stop running, it may take a few minutes to get your breath back.

oxygen   substance in the air that goes into your body when you breathe
gas   substance that is neither a solid nor a liquid

Speeding up

When you start running, your leg muscles start working harder. So they need more oxygen. You have to breathe faster to get more oxygen into your blood. Your heart beats faster to pump the oxygen to your leg muscles. If you run very fast, you run out of breath!

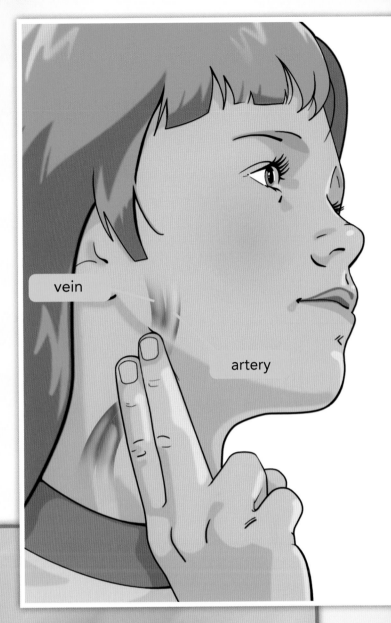

vein

artery

Measure up!

Scientists often measure how fast a sportsperson's heart is beating. The speed is called **heart rate**. You can feel your heart rate. Gently press your fingers into the side of your neck under your chin. The twitches you feel are made by blood being pumped by your heart. Arteries are tubes that carry blood away from the heart. Veins carry blood back to the heart.

lung　　part of your body where air goes when you breathe
heart rate　　how fast your heart is beating

Food for sport

Do you eat extra food if you are going to play a **sport** such as football? When you play sport you need extra **energy** to keep your **muscles** working. The energy comes from **nutrients** in the food you eat.

Some types of food have lots of energy in them. They include pasta, rice, and bread. These contain nutrients called carbohydrates. Energy also comes from foods with natural sugar in them, such as fruit and milk. Your body uses nutrients in food to keep healthy, to repair itself, and to grow.

bread

chicken

Healthy foods help make your body strong and healthy to play sport.

vegetables

energy   something we get from food that lets us do work, such as running
nutrient   substance in food that your body needs to grow and live

Drink lots of water!

You also get thirsty when you play sport. When you run your body gets hot. Water comes out through your skin. This is called sweating. As the water dries up, it cools your body. If your body loses too much water, you can start feeling ill. So you need to drink water when you exercise.

It is important to drink regularly on a long run in warm weather.

Measure up

You might have seen food packages that show information about the food inside. One piece of information is the energy in the food. This is shown in **kilojoules** (KJ) or **kilocalories** (kcal).

kilojoule   measurement of the energy in food (1,000 joules)
kilocalorie measurement of the energy in food (1,000 calories)

11

Pushes and pulls

When you are playing **sport**, you often push or pull on things to make them move. These pushes and pulls are all called **forces**. Forces make things start to move, get faster, slower, and stop. In many sports, you hit a ball with a bat or racket. The bat or racket pushes on the ball, making the ball start moving.

The red arrow shows which way you have to push to throw the ball up and along.

Moving objects

Heavy objects are harder to get moving than objects that are light in weight. Imagine kicking a leather football and a beach ball into a goal. You have to push harder with your foot on the leather football than the beach ball. That is because the leather football is heavier.

In your day

Can you think of pushes and pulls you use in the sports you play? You push on a ball with your hand as you throw it. You push and pull on a tennis racket to swing it. You push on a football with your feet to kick it.

When you hit a tennis ball, the push from the racket squashes the ball.

Action and reaction

Do you like going swimming? Think about pushing off from the side of the pool. Your push on the wall makes you shoot through the water. This happens because the wall pushes back on you. Scientists call the push you make on the wall the **action**. The push the wall makes on you is called the **reaction**.

Pushing on water

Action and reaction also help you to swim along. You pull on the water with your hands, and the water pushes back. This makes you go forwards. The same thing happens in a canoe. When someone pushes on the water with a paddle, the water pushes back. This makes the canoe move.

In your day

Next time you go swimming, think about the science that is happening when you swim. Notice what happens when you push off gently from the side of the pool. Then try pushing off hard. You will notice that you go much further when the push you make on the wall is bigger.

action   movement someone or something makes
reaction   movement that is in the opposite direction to an action

When this swimmer turns around, she pushes off the wall to speed up.

Getting a grip

Rub your hands together. If you press them together hard, it is difficult to make them slide past each other. A **force** called **friction** stops them from sliding.

Friction is very useful in **sport**. Sports shoes have rubbery patterns on their soles that make friction with the ground. This helps the feet grip the ground. Different shoes are designed to grip on grass, athletic tracks, or mud.

When you run, friction between your feet and the ground pushes you forwards.

Friction pushes the runner forwards

Friction between shoe and ground

friction   force caused by two things rubbing together or sliding past each other

Holding tight

Sports gloves help players to grip balls, bats, or other equipment. Goalkeepers wear gloves with rubber palms to help them grip a football. Bats and rackets also have soft rubber grips. Friction between a player's hand and the grip stops the bat or racket from slipping.

Gloves help this man grip his bat.

Stay safe

Friction is really useful, but it can be dangerous. If two things slide past each other very fast, the friction between them can make a lot of heat. Never slide down a rope because the friction could burn your hands.

Sliding and rolling

Friction stops two surfaces that are touching from sliding past each other. It is useful for gripping things. In some sports, however, we need to get rid of friction.

Winter sports such as ice-skating take place on solid ice. Skaters wear boots with narrow metal **blades**. The friction between the ice and the blade is reduced, so the skater can skim along quickly. Luge riders also travel very fast along icy tracks. A luge is a very light sled and it moves along using two parts called runners.

This rider is sliding down a track on his luge.

blade   narrow piece of metal, similar to a knife

Skimming across snow

Skis and snowboards skim across the snow. Their undersides are very smooth and covered with wax. This makes the friction between the skis or snowboard much smaller.

Rubbing the bottom of skis with wax makes the skis slide better on snow.

Wheels reduce friction, too. The wheels on bicycles, skateboards, and roller blades let the rider roll easily along the ground.

Stay safe

You have to be very careful not to slip on steep ice and snow. Mountaineers wear spikes on their boots called crampons. The spikes dig into the ice and snow and make lots of friction.

Moving smoothly

When you want to go fast on your bicycle, do you crouch down with your head close to the handlebars? Do you know why this makes you go faster? It is because the air pushes on you as you cycle through it. The push is called **drag**. It tries to slow you down. When you crouch down, you make the drag smaller.

Drag tries to slow anything that moves along in the air. That includes cyclists, skiers, runners, and objects such as golf balls. To move as fast as possible we try to make drag as small as possible. We do this by using **streamlined** shapes. These are smooth, slim shapes.

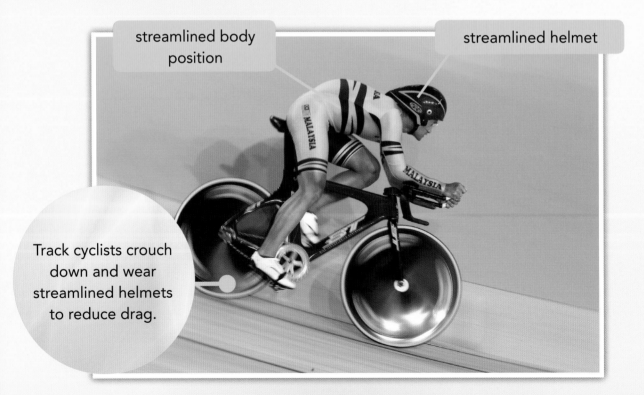

streamlined body position

streamlined helmet

Track cyclists crouch down and wear streamlined helmets to reduce drag.

---

drag   force of air that pushes against objects

Streamlined bodies

Water makes drag as well. Drag pushes against swimmers as they try to swim through the water. So swimmers also try to make their bodies as streamlined as possible.

Making a streamlined shape helps this diver to slide easily into the water.

Stay safe

If a diver hits the water without being streamlined she can hurt herself. Have you ever done a "belly flop"? That is when you dive but land flat on the water, instead of going in head first. It really hurts!

Materials in sport

Take a look at all the different balls, rackets, bats, and other **sports** equipment you have. You will probably see metals, plastics, wood, and **fabrics**.

The materials are chosen because of how strong they are. They are also chosen because of how stretchy or flexible (bendy) they are, or how heavy they are. These are the **properties** of the materials.

Tennis players make use of many different materials in their clothes and equipment.

clothes

shoes

racket

fabric   material that comes in flat sheets and can be bent, such as leather
property   what a material is like (such as how hard it is)

Materials for balls

Footballs are made from layers of plastic and rubber. The plastic on the outside makes the ball tough and shiny. The rubber on the inside stops air escaping. The layers are thin, so the ball is very light. Basketballs are made from rubber. This makes them easy to grip. Baseballs are made from cork. This allows them to be hit very far and high.

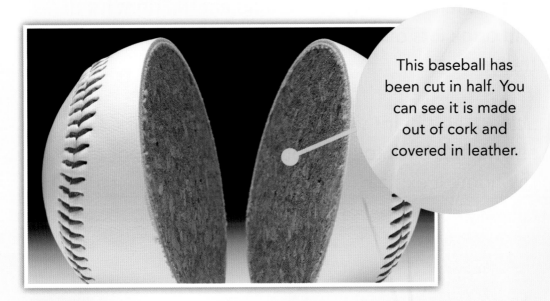

This baseball has been cut in half. You can see it is made out of cork and covered in leather.

In your day
Take a look at the fabrics that your sports clothes are made from. The fabrics are chosen so they feel comfortable next to your skin. They also carry sweat away from your skin and can dry out quickly.

Science in your life

Have you ever played basketball or seen someone else playing it? Think about all the ways science is at work in this **sport**.

Science in basketball

Science explains how your **skeleton** and **muscles** move so you can run, catch, and throw the basketball.

Science tells you why you should eat the right foods and drink lots of water if you want to be able to play the game.

Science also helps you understand why a basketball always falls back to the ground after you shoot towards the hoop. It explains why basketball players wear special boots with soft, rubbery soles. Lastly, it explains why a basketball has a pimpled, rubber surface.

In your day

Next time you watch your favourite sport, try to think about the science that is happening. What **forces** are making the players move about? What special materials are being used?

Did you realize there was so much science going on when you play sport and games?

Try it yourself

Test how high different balls bounce

Balls are part of many different **sports**. There are footballs, tennis balls, cricket balls, golf balls, and baseballs. All these balls are made from different materials. Some are quite soft, and some are hard. They are all made to bounce just the right amount for the sport they are used in.

Try this experiment to find out how high different balls bounce.

What you need:

- different balls used for sports (for example, a tennis ball, golf ball, football, and basketball)
- paper
- sticky tape
- paper and pencil

What to do:

1. Make a strip of paper 1 metre (40 inches) long x 20 centimetres (8 inches) wide, by attaching sheets of paper together.

2. In a room with a solid floor (either concrete or tiles), stick the strip of paper on a wall or door. One end must touch the floor. Ask an adult to help you.

3. Hold the first ball level with the top of the paper strip. Drop it and watch carefully how high it bounces. Make a mark on the strip of paper level with the highest point the ball reached. Write the name of the ball next to the mark.

4. Repeat step 3 with the other balls you have.

Which ball bounced the highest? Think about why each ball is designed to bounce as high as it does.

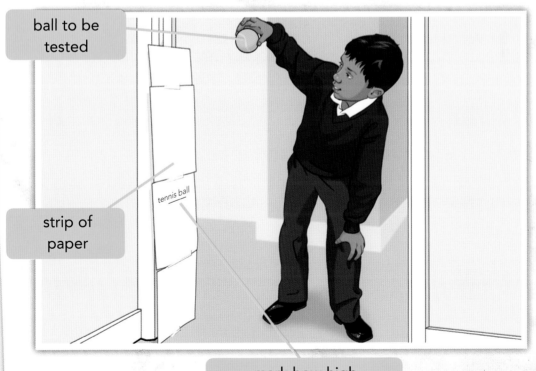

ball to be tested

strip of paper

tennis ball

mark how high the ball bounces

Glossary

action movement someone or something makes

blade narrow piece of metal, similar to a knife

drag force of air that pushes against objects

energy something we get from food that lets us do work, such as running

fabric material that comes in flat sheets and can be bent, such as leather

force push or pull that makes things move

friction force caused by two things rubbing together or sliding past each other

gas substance that is neither a liquid nor a solid

gravity force that pulls things down to the ground

heart rate how fast your heart is beating

joint place where two bones meet and your skeleton can bend

kilojoule measurement of the energy in food (1,000 joules)

kilocalorie measurement of the energy in food (1,000 calories)

lung part of your body where air goes when you breathe

muscle part of your body that makes your skeleton bend and move

nutrient substance in food that your body needs to grow and live

oxygen substance in the air that goes into your body when you breathe

property what a material is like (such as how hard it is)

reaction movement that is in the opposite direction to an action

skeleton frame of bones that supports your body

sport activity that needs fitness or skill

sportspeople people who play sports

streamlined if something is streamlined, it has a smooth, slim shape that helps it move more easily

Find out more

Use these resources to find more fun and useful information about the science behind sport.

Books

Basketball (The Science of Sport), Suzanne Slade (Raintree, 2011)

Football (Sports Science), Natalie Hyde (Franklin Watts, 2009)

Gravity (Fantastic Forces), Chris Oxlade (Heinemann Library, 2007)

How Do My Muscles Get Strong? (Inside My Body), Steve Parker (Raintree, 2011)

Secrets of Sport (Extreme Science), James de Winter (A&C Black, 2009)

Sports Science (Why Science Matters), Andrew Solway (Heinemann LIbrary, 2010)

Sports Technology (Cool Science), Ron Fridell (Lerner Books, 2009)

Websites

news.bbc.co.uk/cbbcnews/hi/sport/default.stm
Take a look at this website to find out what is happening in your favourite sport.

www.bbc.co.uk/schools/ks2bitesize/science/physical_processes/friction/play.shtml
Visit this website to do a really fun interactive activity that will help you learn more about friction.

www.engineeringinteract.org/applications.htm
Watch the slides on this website to find out lots more about forces.

www.childrenfirst.nhs.uk/kids/health/eat_smart/
Learn about all the different ways you can help your body grow strong and healthy – and visit Poo Corner to find out what your poo says about you!

www.childrenfirst.nhs.uk/kids/health/eat_smart/exercise_centre/index.html
If you think sport and excercise are not for you, visit this website for some easy tips on getting fit.

Index